Healing Your Marriage
by Healing Yourself

Healing Your Marriage by Healing Yourself

Salima Sanford

Mistletoe Press

Design by Meadowlark Publishing Services.

Cover and interior illustrations by Patty Schork Wear.

Author photo courtesy of the author.

Published by Mistletoe Press.

Manufactured in the United States of America.

ISBN 979-8-9855111-0-9

Published 2022

Contents

Preface

This book, begun as a master's thesis for the University of Spiritual Healing and Sufism (USHS) in 2009, was first published in 2011. It has since been trimmed down and additional teachings added for the 2015 edition.

This book is intended for anyone experiencing marital (or any core relationship) challenges, particularly of a volatile nature. Some of the suggestions may appear martyr-like, due to the dedication to personal work that is recommended. However, without self-responsibility and generosity, love cannot fully blossom. In the end, the real winner is the one who stays with the challenges of marriage and is gifted with the qualities of strength, patience, tolerance, compassion, and love that naturally ensue.

Acknowledgments

I am deeply grateful to my guide, Sidi Shaykh Muhammad Sa'id al-Jamal ar-Rifa'i ash-Shadhuli, for his ever-present love and support and for the inspirational richness of his writings. Were it not for hearing his call, I might not have found my way back to God, to Whom my ultimate gratitude and indebtedness belong.

I will be forever grateful to my beloved husband, Graham, for staying the course with our marriage in spite of the difficulties we have encountered. His steadfast nature is gradually melting my heart and unveiling the truth that love can and will endure.

May Allah bless all who find these pages and may He forgive me for any words that do not deliver clear water for the hearts of readers.

Introduction

But if in your fear you would seek only love's peace and love's pleasure, then it is better for you that you cover your nakedness and pass out of love's threshing-floor, into the seasonless world where you shall laugh, but not all of your laughter, and weep, but not all of your tears.

—Kahil Gibran, The Prophet

In the commitment of marriage we find both our greatest joy and our deepest struggles. The intimacy of marriage places us uncomfortably face-to-face with our truest selves to such an extent that many of us give up on marriage, not for lack of love, but because our challenges and apparent failures become overwhelming.

In truth, it is not so much about whom we marry, as what the marriage invites us to learn about ourselves. Therefore, this book's focus is on the reader's relationship with his or her own self, guiding the reader, *inshallah,** to develop skills and attitudes that will strengthen all relationships.

---

*   God willing

1

Preparing Yourself and Your Environment

*What keeps us alive, what allows us
to endure?
I think it is the hope of loving or being loved.*[1]

Assessing Your Marriage

If you are reading this book, you are likely experiencing difficult challenges in your marriage or another significant relationship. Although your partner is not the focus of this book, it will be helpful to first acknowledge your opinions about him or her, in order to move beyond them.

The Negatives

To begin with, make a list of those things that your spouse does, or traits that he or she exhibits, that you consider detrimental to your relationship and impediments to its improvement.[2] Ironically, the exercise of bringing your negative thoughts into the open may actually facilitate their release.

It is necessary to make a *written* list, as you will be using it for the next exercise. Allow enough time to exhaust your concerns.

When you are finished, slowly read aloud each item on your list. Allow your insights and emotional reactions to percolate into consciousness. *As you look over each item a second time, honestly ask yourself:*

- *Is this a trait in myself that perhaps I don't recognize or that I struggle to inhibit?*
- *Is this a trait I could admire if it were in moderation? (such as frugality vs. stinginess)*
- *Do I have unpleasant memories of someone else who had this trait?*
- *Is this behavior common to other significant persons in my life, past or present?*
- *Where I have listed an opinion, do I hold a similar opinion of other people in my life?*

- *What judgments or inferences am I making about my spouse based on my observations of this behavior?*

Record your responses. They may prove helpful later. Please, this information is just for your own eyes. Some of your feelings and revelations are in their infancy. This is not the time for sharing. Your challenges are real, but over time you will see that your feelings and discomforts are as much about *you* as they are about your spouse.

The truth is that the more intimacy grows, the more you will realize that your partner is your perfect mirror, reflecting not only your beautiful qualities, but also your less desirable nature. Intimate relationship inevitably stirs up old memories and strong beliefs, but only because they are ready for transformation.

The Positives

Now write down everything you love and admire about your partner.[3] When you finish, read the list aloud and appreciate that what you admire in your partner also mirrors your best self, or you would not be able to recognize the trait in him or her!

Habitual Behaviors

As a last exercise, observe the nature of the friction between you and your partner. Notice if there is a particular time of day or situation that makes arguments more likely and whether you have a habitual way of responding that seems to perpetuate disagreements or misunderstandings.

In my marriage, for example, I began to notice that at least half of our arguments occurred over the breakfast table. As communication improved between us, I was able to make a suggestion (as a scientific experiment) that we take a quick shower upon awakening, to wash off any emotions accumulated during the night, and then sit in our spare room for ten minutes before going down for breakfast. It actually worked to prevent breakfast tension. After a while we stopped this ritual, but whenever arguing starts up again, we return to this process, knowing that it works for us.

The next time you face a challenging moment in your marriage, *respond differently* and observe what happens. Changing your manner of response will change the nature of the interaction. Through observations of the results, you may discover new behaviors that can thwart old negative habits. For example, if your style is to point out your spouse's "mistakes," then instead remain calm and silent. If you usually remain present and silent, then excuse yourself and slip off to be alone for a while. You always have the freedom to change your manner of interaction, with the intention of attending to *your* needs while remaining, to the best of your ability, gentle with your partner. In this way you participate positively in the evolution of the relationship.

Addressing the Ego

I said, "Why do you cut me with your sharp words?"
(God) said, "My words wouldn't hurt you if you
weren't in love with yourself."
—*Rumi*

The self that Rumi refers to in this poem is the ego self, not the spiritual self. When our animalistic self is in charge, we may become *ruled* by persistent inner voices, such as *"I must have that,"* *"I deserve better,"* or *"Everyone else does it,"* i.e., the "I-want-what-I want" part of the self. It is fine to have wants; it is this passion that drives us. But we won't always get what we want, and this is where we can learn to discipline our ego.

One way we are reminded that our ego has gotten the upper hand is through the reactions of others, reactions that may not always feel so good. The critical choice in those moments is whether we turn to God for help or to our defensive and domineering egos. We can learn, through awareness and prayer, to allow harsh words to humble us and elicit our compassion, rather than cripple and shame us. This does not mean we must lose our strength, only our arrogance.

It is vital to discipline our bodies and thoughts, because out-of-control egos provide entry points for darker thoughts and compulsions to come in, such as obsession, depression, or hopelessness.

Spiritual pursuits help to tame and balance our appetites by feeding us on a more deeply sustaining level than the momentary fulfillment of our ego-desires. With body and spirit working together, we can begin to make choices that are more closely aligned with God's guidance. As the once-demanding voice of our ego becomes quieter, we may now begin to hear the voice of our soul's longing and wisdom.

Sanctuary

> *Be still and know that I am God.*
> —*Psalm 46:10*

It is essential to your spiritual walking to find a safe place where you can be alone and undisturbed. This could be a small room, a walk-in closet, a corner that can be screened off, or even a tree or rock, weather permitting.

Give your sanctuary a name: e.g., the prayer room, the meditation room, the green room, so you can tell your family members where you are going when you need some time alone. If they are prone to concern, they will worry less if, in advance of entering, you give an estimate as to about how long you will be there and, if it feels right, what your intent is. Most spouses will be reassured by being told that you are going off to work on your anger or grief, especially if they later observe you emerging a calmer, happier person.

A sanctuary is not only a place for strong emotions to be felt and healed, but also a place for sitting and allowing your spirit to be nurtured. It is extremely helpful to spend time each day sitting quietly, checking in with your heart, mind, and body. Morning visits to your quiet place permit you to release any discomforts accumulated from dreams or sleeping difficulties, and to set the tone for the day. In the evenings you may wish to reflect on the day, considering, for example, what you are grateful for and what you did well or seeking forgiveness for any actions you may regret. Sitting in stillness can help you return to what my older sister calls *a state of grace.* You will incrementally return to your divine self, the self once buried by debris from life's struggles.

You are not at peace because you are in conflict inside. This is understandable, as we have awareness on so many levels—heart, mind, spirit, worldly activities. Maybe your heart and head are not working in unison. Perhaps you have a strong feeling that you persistently ignore, such as grief or anger, because you do not yet have the tools for dealing with it alone. Examine your inner voices. Are they helpful? If not, encourage, instead, the inner voices that unite all the parts of yourself and make you feel safe, peaceful, and loved.

Family members may begin to use your sanctuary as well. This is because you have set a precedent of honoring the universal need for a place for peaceful reflection. As the security provided by your sanctuary begins to *take root inside of you*, it may be okay with you if others enter your space, providing they honor it. Every family member has visited my prayer room at one time or another. You may wish to establish simple rules for the space, such as shoes off or quiet speech, though not at the expense of others' feelings. Eventually, the room itself will develop an energy that invites respect and quiet reflection.

Self-Knowledge
Self-knowledge, borne of self-reflection, is knowledge of God. Almost every tradition echoes this refrain.

It is a sad fate for a man to die too well known to everybody else, and still unknown to himself.
—*Francis Bacon*

He who knows himself, knows his Lord.
—*Ascribed to Prophet Mohammad*

The very self of a being is that mystery which is known only to it and to God.
—*Ibn al-Arabi,* The Ringstones of Wisdom

The fully awakened soul of man expresses every
Divine Quality in a single, living self.
—*Ibn Al-Arabi,* The Ringstones of Wisdom

Self-Assessment

Codependency
One of the great challenges in marriage is to stay true to yourself while honoring your spouse. Many people err to one extreme or another, either doing as they wish, as if living alone, or giving up all their rights to please their mate. Either extreme can breed resentment and cause separation from your partner.

The ideal relationship is one where both partners feel safe enough to remain vulnerable and to explore and care for their truest selves; they have been able to establish personal boundaries that allow for both intimacy and personal space.

Avoid being at the whim of your spouse's moods, however strong they may be. If you make every decision in your relationship based on what you think your spouse needs, you may soon lose touch with your own needs. Moreover, if your primary focus is on someone else rather than on your personal growth, you are, in a sense, making a god of that person.

For example, when I make decisions based on an attempt to manipulate my husband's moods, I'm unconsciously assuming that I can, and should, control who he is. (I may even be drastically misinterpreting his behavior in the first place.) Making him the prime focus of my life does not promote a healthy relationship. Rather, it limits freedom for us both.

We all carry the potential to be fully realized human beings. Unplug yourself from others. Gather yourself back up and plug into God alone. This advice is also helpful in relationships with grown children. The very real pain of separation from our children as they mature, sometimes referred to as the empty nest syndrome, can be relieved if we but claim those parts of ourselves we have been asking our children to carry for us.

For example, you may be dependent on the nearness of your son because of his kindness and passion for life. Since his moving into his own life is inevitable, the real medicine for your heart is to find and grow your own kindness, your own passion. In this way you become a more contented and whole person. As an integrated, independent being, your relationship with your son may become more mutually enriching, not simply a substitution for what you lack.

Not all types of dependency lead to codependency. Men and women naturally depend on one another. A woman often needs the man to protect and comfort her, to be there for her. A man often needs unconditional love and assurances that he is a good provider. Don't become so vigilant about codependency that you forget to say, *I need you.* Such a heartfelt request will most always soften the heart of your spouse.

Pictures, Voices, and Veils

Pictures are recollections of pivotal events in your life that are still affecting you, primarily because of unresolved issues related to the events. Emotions become attached to these critical memories at the time of their formation. Thus, incidents in the present that appear similar to these past events can trigger the reoccurrence of old emotions and reactions.

Let's take the hypothetical example of someone we'll call Ellen. Let's suppose, for example, that as a child, Ellen's mother was easily stressed, which frequently led to her being angry and attacking Ellen verbally, sometime even physically. Ellen may still retain an image, a *picture,* of a particular event (or events) when her mother was stressed and angry. As a result, whenever she sees someone becoming stressed, she assumes they will become angry, and possibly hurtful. When she senses tension in a person, her association of stress with ensuing anger will result in emotional, even physical pain; e.g., her stomach may clench exactly as if someone had punched her. Because most people become stressed at one time or another, her heightened response will be affecting most of her relationships.

We all carry images from our past, sometimes

hidden to us, that affect our present behavior and how we feel about our selves. Through awareness and healing work, we can begin to see behind our pictures to the truth: that although a present situation may *resemble* a given memory, it is *not* a repeat of the same experience. Through this growing awareness, our habitual response patterns can begin to change.

As we begin to recollect these active images, we set foot on the road to healing. It may be that the underlying images (and our accompanying unmet needs) are not yet clear to us, only the fact that certain types of behaviors presented by others are terribly upsetting to us, beyond what is warranted by the situation.

Instead of going into blame or resistance each time we *are* upset, it helps to spend some time alone sorting things out. First, we must be sure to comfort ourselves. Everyone has triggers and everyone at one time or another finds themselves at the mercy of events that stir up long-held unhappy memories.

When you recognize situations that routinely trigger your emotions, it may be helpful to explore your feelings and the images that come up. In your quiet space, search for memories of past events that generated similar feelings and responses to what you are now experiencing. Perhaps you recall images of similar situations from childhood. Voices, such as "I can't do anything right" or I don't deserve this" may tag along. These images and voices may easily dominate your thoughts and actions if their falsehood is not recognized.

To continue with the hypothetical example, a voice accompanying Ellen's *picture* might be *"I'd better be careful not to make anyone angry or I'll get hurt."* When she was young, this voice *protected* her by reminding her to stay away from her mother when she was angry, but now that she is an adult it may result in her avoiding or overreacting to conflict.

At the root of the voice will be an equally unreliable *belief*. Ellen may have come to believe that she is worthless because of the anger dumped on her as a child. Even now she may think people are always mad at her (even when they are not), which, of course, validates her belief in her unworthiness. Perhaps she doesn't even allow herself to feel anger, much less express it, believing that anger, disagreement, even self-assertion, are inherently *wrong*. Denying herself, and others, the essential human emotion of anger prevents her from becoming a fully developed person, capable of unflinchingly facing the challenges of an intimate relationship.

Continuing with the example of Ellen, in the face of her spouse's stress or anger she will probably show fear, withdrawal, and disapproval instead of love, acceptance, and understanding. As a result, her spouse's anger will likely intensify when he sees himself through her eyes. Her belief that anger is bad is a veil, because it veils or blocks her clear understanding of situations.

With effort, if that is one's goal, a person can learn to deal with and eventually lose his or her fear of anger. Through identifying and understanding the causes of one's own triggers, it becomes easier to recognize the fear and hurt beneath a spouse's anger, and to feel compassion, even endearment, instead of fear.

At USHS* we were once asked to write our personal "story" in *one* short paragraph and to give it a title. My roommate's title, encapsulating her life story, was *Fear Factor*; mine was *I Don't Deserve This!* As we shared our stories we could see the infinite variety of limitations placed on each of us by the baggage of our history, none of them merited by present conditions. Over time, I began to see how often my actions were based on my belief that I deserved better. In other words, I was not in acceptance, much less appreciation, of what God was giving me. This realization was a doorway for exiting the prison of my story.

Through spiritual work, the emotions tied up in your memories can be released permanently so that, miraculously, when the images are recalled, the old feelings and reactions no longer accompany them, much like being able to listen to an old love song

---

*   University of Spiritual Healing and Sufism, http://sufiuniversity.org/

without it tugging at your heart. When the pictures lose their hold on you, the associated ill-serving voices and beliefs also fall away, freeing you to move on from your past and to open to receive what your being truly needs in the present.

Try writing and titling your own story. It won't take long! Reducing your entire history to a single paragraph will minimize its importance and help you to remember that *who you are now need not be defined or limited by what happened to you in the past.*

In summary, through recognizing and detaching from any unhelpful pictures, voices, and beliefs, our past history need not inappropriately drive our present behavior. As we allow God to lift these veils, we will begin to blossom as the special person we are, a divine being once veiled by the impact of life events.

Veils of Light

Besides veils of negativity, there are more subtle veils that also block your progress, referred to as *veils of light.* For example, as you become a more loving person because of your spiritual work, you can easily become veiled by this new image of yourself. You may then fall into self-satisfaction, which precludes the need for further spiritual walking.

With regards to marriage, a veil of light might be your picture of how you think your marriage should be. For example, you may believe that you should always feel love, should never lose your temper, and should always treat one another as sacred beings. (Notice the *should*, an unhelpful word.) These beliefs of how you both ought to behave turn you away from love in the name of what appears to be honorable intention. Your ideas seem correct, yet in effect, you are trying to control the evolution of your marriage rather than letting it grow naturally, however untidily!

As an experiment in releasing your current pictures, when you wake up tomorrow try noticing your spouse as if seeing him or her for the first time. Banish all thoughts and pictures of who you think he or she is, or what behavior you expect to see. (Yes, you *can* do this.) Greet your spouse with a clean slate. You may be pleasantly surprised by the results.

When you relate to one another as static beings, you limit each other's capacity for growth. When you leave the past behind and embrace the unlimited potential of one another, you give one another the gift of freedom. Move into unknown territory. Surrender to what God makes for you, rather than continually struggle to make things happen your way.

The Gifts in the Challenges

So be patient in times of constriction and
bear its heat because in this heat is countless
and limitless wisdom.[4]

It takes courage, when one is emotionally "triggered," to see a challenging situation as an *opportunity* for releasing the pain of old wounds. Sometimes you may feel that your difficulties are more than you can handle, and so you remain blind to them, blame others, or pretend you are not suffering inside. However, there is truth to the adage that you are not given more than you can bear. Well, it may be more than you can bear *alone*, but not more than you can bear if you call upon God, which is probably the point.

A counselor once told me that every tear I had blocked in my life would eventually need to come out. Marriage has been very helpful with this! There seems to be no end to my tears, yet I am learning how to let the tears flow when they come, without ascribing meaning to or dramatizing them. Sometimes rage is released before the tears, a feeling I might never have known and worked through were it not for the challenges of marriage. Our spouses are most frequently the ones who trigger our emotions, but they are also our greatest source of love. Within the container of marriage we can find the healing that only comes when we face our deepest fears and pain. *Alhamdulillah* (All praise to God)!

Being in the intimacy of marriage exposes your darkest thoughts and outmoded beliefs because it is inevitable that *as you open your heart to your spouse your wounds are also exposed,* touching the very core of your insecurities. This is one of the threats of marriage and also its greatest blessing, for in marriage you are given endless opportunities to do spiritual work on the parts of you that need it the most.

The Qur'an has a passage that reads, *"and with difficulty comes ease, and with difficulty comes ease* (Qur'an 95:5–6)."* Hidden within every challenging situation is a gift. Perhaps you are in need of more patience and your teenager forgets to call to say he will be late, or you are in need of greater humility and you are sharply criticized or fail at a task. I often marvel at how perfectly each of my friends' difficulties have been suited to what she most fears. The friend who worried about money had a financial scare, my devout friend's husband decided he was an atheist, and my heart longed for peace but my house was a constant battlefield. Yet for each one of us, these challenges were the doorways to greater freedom when we accepted our situation, turned unflinchingly inward to discern God's teaching, and did the much-needed personal work.

For example, I used to wonder why my spouse was so rude to me. *Surely I don't deserve this,* I thought. Acting not from my story, but from knowing that my relationship with my husband is a mirror of my relationship with God, I searched through inspirational books for how to be more polite with God. I found a beautiful paragraph on etiquette in prayer. Here is an excerpt from that reading:

> *(Prayer) is one of the highest forms of worship, for the act in itself is a demonstration of the worshipper's absolute reliance on God alone.... The worshipper is raising his hands up, and in a state of utter humility and dependence on His Lord and Sustainer, he is beseeching God to help him, to guide him, to cure him, to draw him close... Prayer is a deeply sacred practice, for it goes beyond the obligations, into a deep sense of connection and surrender to our*
> *Lord, and is a constant affirmation in our faith in His Mercy.*[5]

Being moved by this reading, I was inspired to enter into a place of deeper courtesy and respect in prayer. As I made an effort to practice greater courtesy in my relationship with God, it naturally followed that I held others and myself in greater reverence, because how we live is also a form of prayer. Miraculously, as I focused on my own politeness, my husband's rudeness began to fall away.

The truth is that when *you* change inside, people around you also change. The lesson is, *strive to become what you want to see in others.*

Humility

It should be a relief to realize you are not in charge of your life. Yes, you have free will, but you also have little control over what life brings your way. Perhaps you haven't done such a great job of self-management anyway. And yet your mistakes have been essential, because through them you have learned how you do not want to live.

If you really want to feel humility, then mess up totally! For example, can you recall a circumstance when you were pushy and judgmental with your spouse and you later (sheepishly) realized that he or she had acted with greater patience and integrity than you? Did you feel greater compassion and respect for your partner afterward? Was that realization freeing? Were you merciful with yourself? If your answers were *yes, yes, and yes,* then you are learning from your mistakes!

Be forgiving with yourself. Mistakes define the boundaries of one's spiritual path and remind us of our humanity. Each setback is an opportunity for learning. When you recognize that you did not live up to your expectations, *allow the feeling of regret,* because this opens the door for God's mercy to flow in. Then, to each interaction that follows you will bring a greater kindness and vulnerability. In this way you begin to taste the sweetness of humility.

Whatever your pictures are of the perfect marriage, let them go, for *"when (love) speaks to you believe in him, though his voice may shatter your dreams as the north wind lays waste the garden."*[6]

By abandoning your agenda and accepting that your dreams will be shattered, you open the doorway for a new creation in your marriage and allow it to flower naturally with a unique fragrance, perhaps imperfect, but no less beautiful for that.

Mirroring

Have you ever noticed, when you are grocery shopping, for example, that if you arrive at the store irritable, the lines move slowly, the cashier is unfriendly, and you have a pretty miserable experience most of the time? Conversely, when your day has gone well and your heart is filled with love for mankind and gratitude for life you usually have a more positive experience. The people you see are smiling, and perhaps your presence brings joy to others.

In his book *The Reality of Gnosis*, Sidi al-Jamal writes that *everything* you witness is "from you and for you." From this place whoever sees good, let him praise God, "but if he sees otherwise, let him only blame himself. If you see a shortcoming … then know that it is your own shortcoming" and "work to remove this shortcoming from yourself and you will not see its trace." In truth, if we want anyone's image to be more pleasant, then ours must become more pleasant first.

God mirrors yourself back to you. Events don't happen *to* you so much as they happen *from* you. For example, if you carry the quality of deep mercy, your life will be surrounded with mercy. You will more often witness the kindness of others, hear the sweetness of the bird's song, glimpse the tenderness of a mother's love. If you carry hate, you will more likely see hate, anger, and mistrust around you.

Naturally you will be tested by life events. It may be that life brings you a challenging experience in order to strengthen a quality in you: e.g., to shine light on where you might be more merciful, helping you understand the deeper subtleties of mercy. Conversely the world may reflect for you only beauty and kindness in order to melt your hate, to open your heart to another way of being. We are in every moment being walked closer by a merciful and understanding God.

It is not uncommon to experience a similar type of problem throughout our life until we get the message, the learning from it. For example, since childhood I have repeatedly encountered angry people, while I always *appeared* to be mild mannered. The awakening for me was the day the enormous rage I unknowingly held inside finally exploded. (I suppose it was because I had begun to feel some degree of safety in my marriage.) In that moment I could no longer run from my husband's anger, nor could I tolerate it a moment longer, and my sweet façade crumbled. The person who emerged shocked us both.

In truth, the entire dynamics of our volatile marriage has been perfectly designed to illuminate, release, and heal the deep-seated anger we both carry from childhood. (Our counselor says we are the "perfect mirrors" for one another.) Since that awakening, we have been "working on ourselves" in differing ways and at differing speeds (the work is never done). We at least understand now that when anger presents to us, it is a reflection of our own inner being. Therefore, in response, we focus on ourselves, not on what the other has done.

Therein lies our teaching and our healing.

What you judge, you are; when you are judgmental about someone else's behavior, you are most likely in denial about a similar aspect in your self. While I sometimes forget, I have come to realize that every bothersome trait I perceive in my husband is a trait I also carry. Maybe this trait that triggers me is repressed, or I have it to a lesser degree, or I act differently but out of the same need. I wouldn't be bothered by the trait in him unless the behavior was related to me in some respect, much as a tuning fork resonates with a matching vibrational frequency.

By all outward appearances, your spouse may mirror the exact opposite of your normal behavior, but it is all *related* to you. To help me understand this, my counselor suggested that I draw a line, a continuum similar to a number line, but labeled with feelings. Starting from the far left I wrote the word "rage." Then, at even intervals, I wrote "anger," then "irritation," and then "frustration." The midline was labeled "vulnerability." Moving to the right were the words "confusion," "separation," "fear," and on the far right, "terror." It will help if you draw this out for yourself.

How does this apply to our meltdowns? Let's say that my husband reacts to something I say or do by moving left from the vulnerable midline of this continuum, just a notch, say, into *frustration*. I have a choice. I can stay vulnerable and in reliance on God for support, or I can automatically move a similar degree in the opposite direction, to *confusion*. That will likely trigger him further, into *irritation*, and if I remain unconscious, I will move into painful *separation*. He may then move quickly to *anger*, and so I move into *fear*, and so on, in an emotional game of ping-pong.

Thus, the only way to stay connected with our partners is to remain conscious and vulnerable. *Acting unconsciously, we are slaves to our voices, our pictures, and our emotions.*

The concept of mirroring becomes really interesting if taken a step further. My counselor has suggested that my spouse, in his movement toward anger, may be mirroring the very emotion I habitually repress or deny. In other words, his anger reflects my unacknowledged anger. Conversely, my fear reflects the fear that he has long denied.

To put it differently, underlying his anger is his own fear; beneath my manifest fear is repressed anger. In fact, when we go the fullest extreme, as we used to, we finally flip sides—I go into rage and he flees the house in fear. Slaves to our reactions, we used to live in a virtual emotional prison that prevented us from fully participating in life. Believing that it was the other who continually put us in this prison, we avoided any situation that aroused uncomfortable emotions and so were deprived of the sweet vulnerability of intimacy.

How does this one-sidedness of emotional response come about? Many of us are not comfortable with the whole range of emotions, perhaps being denied certain emotions as children, so we have settled into one mode of reacting to discomfort, usually anger or fear. In our lives, then, we will continue to encounter people who strongly reflect our denied feelings, *until we reclaim them.* As we begin to accept and develop the whole range of our human emotions, we will come into greater harmony with ourselves and be better able to sustain the vulnerability required for intimacy.

Other Aspects of Mirroring

Another nuance of mirroring is that it can serve to awaken a part of your better self that you are denying. For example, if someone appears to demean me, that is to say I feel demeaned by his or her behavior, this does not necessarily mean that I demean others or that I need to be taken down a notch. Perhaps I routinely demean myself and the event is providing an opportunity for me to see where I am not recognizing my own worth. I may have a lingering image from the past that still negatively affects my self-worth. Feeling demeaned by someone shows me, in my strong reaction, that this is *not* a true image, thus allowing me to begin to feel my self-worth and honor that.

Finally, another's words or actions may evoke latent qualities in me that are appropriate to the situation. For example, I may be a bit short on compassion and, ironically, I find myself continually in situations that warrant compassionate action. Instead of reacting in frustration and impatience, I can consciously allow (and pray for!) compassion to well up inside of me and flow outward to others. In this way, instead of battling my experience, I can let the behavior of others, however challenging, evoke higher qualities that lie within me. Moreover, when these qualities emerge, the other person may see him- or herself reflected in me, and thus also find those qualities within!

In an intimate relationship, balance will always

be maintained. Therefore, both partners will be equally extreme or, better still, equally moderate. For example, if one errs financially on the side of miserliness, the other will likely overspend. To the extent that one partner is excessively gregarious, that is to say cannot stand to be alone, the other will veer to the side of reclusiveness. Or, as we have seen, if one is always angry, the other is always fearful. These are not conscious decisions people make. It is just that the overall balance seems to be naturally maintained in a marriage.

However fanciful this may sound, if you observe closely, you will notice that this bears out. In your marriage, any extreme behavior your partner exhibits will lessen when you become more moderate with respect to that behavior. Moreover, when you become more moderate in any arena, a variety of people in your close circle of loved ones may also begin to moderate, shifting in whatever direction leads them to greater balance.

For example, I had a recent epiphany through which I became deeply committed to and even more in love with my spouse. Not only did my husband immediately draw closer to me, but my son suddenly found complete certainty in his intimate relationship, something he said he had never known. Both persons shifted without my sharing a word of my own experience.

This recognition of relationship as a mirror provides countless teachings to help us gain knowledge of ourselves. Through this awareness, we can begin to realize that all interactions, especially intimate ones, are opportunities for our moving into closer relationship with our best selves, and with God. Or as one of my USHS teachers recently wrote, *"My experience is that nothing moves that is not a mirror which perfects our own qualities."*

As our vision clears, we may begin to more clearly see God's presence as Teacher, Guide, and Friend in all that happens. Marriage provides a superb opportunity to uncover the wholeness and divinity of your being. Although living with your perfect mirror in a marriage can be very uncomfortable, it is also a powerful agent for personal growth, because in the places where you still clash with your spouse reside parts of yourself that are ready for cleaning. For this reason, it is often said that marriage is like a rock tumbler, smoothing down the rough edges of both hearts.

2

Assuming
Self-Responsibility

*Move from seeing people as the source
of the difficulty to seeing the place in
yourself that is creating the
difficulty. When you sit with yourself
in responsibility and deep politeness
then you see both your own beauty
and your shortcomings. When you
begin to taste this, the secret light
that you are becomes the source of
your experience.*[1]

Ironically, the way to rekindle love in your marriage is by looking inside yourself rather than focusing on your relationship. In doing so, you will actually forge a stronger union. Why? Because your struggles with your partner are primarily manifestations of the struggles within yourself. Put differently, when you are more comfortable with yourself, you will be more comfortable in your marriage.

Stop Giving Advice

You can be right or you can be in the love. Because you know what has helped you, it is easy to believe that by sharing your wisdom you can solve your spouse's "problem," but this is not the case. Why not? Surely if he or she would just listen to your advice, you could be done with the quarreling!

Look at your intent, however. Do you want simply to "fix" your spouse so that you can go about your business in peace, minus those disturbing habits of his or hers?

Observe the degree of kindness in your words as you speak. Is it ever kind to point out the fault of another? As Sidi al-Jamal writes in *Music of the Soul*,[2] if you "blame and object to him (or her) then his (mistake) becomes visible because of your hardness." If you are "obliged to help others, you will adopt a better way in which you will *remain unchanged within*, yet at the same time" stop the mistake "by your kind judgment" and "understanding."

Strive to cultivate the qualities of kindness, gentleness and understanding. There is strength in these qualities, not weakness. You may have found something great that works for you, and want desperately for your partner to have the same benefits, but unsolicited advice, cloaked in helpfulness, is seldom productive. In fact, such interference will create separation between you. Isn't it connection that you seek?

> *Oh you people! Surely We have created you from a man and a woman and made you peoples and tribes, so that you might come to know one another.*
> —Qur'an 39:16

God guides us all toward goodness and knowing, but the ways are as many as there are people. Everyone has their own path, their own speed of learning, and their own special fragrance. A person's apparent resistance to God's guidance will not be altered by your words, but only by your own reflection of God's light.

If your spouse is doing something you have a negative opinion about, look to yourself to see where you are doing something similar. For example, a few years ago I was very worried about a family member who I believed had an addiction.

The realization that broke my mind and heart open was that I also had an addiction—an addiction to him!* I knew *that* was the only addiction I could control. When I turned to working on myself, rather than trying to control him, we began to communicate. My preaching alienated him. My self-awareness reopened the door to love.

More recently I found myself again worrying that this same person was on the "wrong" path. I was reminded of a story that has always brought me to tears. It is the image of Noah sailing off in the ark with his son remaining on the land, telling his father that all was okay, that he could get to higher ground on his own. This time, I saw the mirror of that young man in me. What took me out of my detrimental judgments was the realization of all the times in which *I* think that I can find my way to higher ground without the guidance of God. This is the only behavior that I can address.

Remaining patient in the presence of what feels like wrong behavior on the part of someone you love is not easy. Our old ways of thinking die hard. However, you simply cannot know the truth for another person, or dictate the path they should be on. It is hard enough knowing your own truth. For each of us, our mistakes are a *vital* part of our healing process.

I have a prayer I do every morning that helps

---

*   This realization came from listening to Byron Katie's recordings of *Loving What Is.*

me enormously. *Dear God, please help me to release my husband into Your care. Forgive me anything I may have done that has hurt him. Help him to forgive me my mistakes and to forgive himself for his mistakes. Please hold him in safety, and give him all that his heart needs.* Then I repeat the prayer for each of my children.

Self-Responsibility

When you no longer expect your mate to provide fully and consistently what you need, you will cease to be a victim in your relationship. Take responsibility for your feelings in the certainty that you alone are responsible for them. Others cannot give you any pain that is not already dwelling inside you (and *vice versa*). Blaming others only stifles love and trust.

For example, if your spouse is critical of you, you may with good intention respond with what you think is patience and tolerance. However, beneath your words, you are viewing your spouse as unlikable and yourself as the better person. (You could probably find support from any number of persons who would agree with your thinking!) Or maybe you respond with impatience and, although you later apologize for losing your temper, you feel justified because of your spouse's behavior.

There is no easy way out of the loop of good person vs. bad person, but it is necessary to break through this veil. Thinking negatively about your partner builds a wall of separation between you. Positive thoughts open the door to sweet intimacy.

In short, the words you speak are not as significant as what you believe in your heart. Feigned patience or begrudging tolerance is not enough. Your spouse responds to what you are feeling, regardless of what you say or don't say. If your patience comes not from love, but rather from a desire to manipulate, you can expect problems.

If you feel love, love will manifest. If your desire is to control, you will be controlled by your desire.

The dynamics of any relationship are a delicate dance. As you do your work, the relationship *will* begin to change. As you clean your heart, you clean the heart of the marriage. Forget what you think your partner should be or should do. Instead, rekindle the love in your heart and *allow love, not your agenda, to be your guide.* Direct your energies to working on *your* issues and have faith that over time your relationship will be transformed in ways even better than you can imagine.

In finding your own compassionate heart, you will in turn see the goodness in your spouse. My spouse used to tell the counselor that he wanted me to love him even when he was losing his temper. We all knew this was unlikely, and yet, as my heart began to change, this became possible. Ironically, I had to begin to own, forgive, and receive healing for my own temper first.

As I began to see the hurt beneath my husband's

anger, I realized that one of my blocks to compassion for him was my unwillingness to feel *in myself* what my husband was feeling. Consequently, his feelings overwhelmed me every time and I shut my heart to him when he needed me most. When I acknowledged and cared for my similar feelings, I gradually came to see his heart more clearly and to find compassion for us both.

Imagine you are both looking at a house in disrepair and then you turn away to view a magnificent sunset. Your spouse will soon turn away from the shambles to witness the sunset with you. Similarly, when you are no longer reflecting on what you don't like about your marriage and instead are witnessing some of its beauty, your spouse will turn his or her witnessing there also, and your hearts will begin to fill with the light of healing.

The Power of Pictures

Instead of making up stories about why your spouse did what he or she did, take care of your reaction. As my neighbor said, people can only give what they know. Giving back anger perpetuates anger. Returning love awakens love in your partner.

Perhaps this story will illustrate how making a picture about an event can perpetuate resentment and close the heart to compassion. Some

time ago I listened to a USHS school recording
from a previous year and soon realized that I was
listening to my own voice. As I listened, I was
uncomfortably taken back to a teaching about
anger during which I had volunteered a current
life event as an example. I heard my shaky voice
describe how I had violently ripped our electric
toothbrush holder off the wall and thrown it to the
floor in anger because my husband was brushing
his teeth and ignoring me while I was talking. I
could feel the tension in the class when I described
what I had done; this was clearly not in keeping
with my seemingly peaceful nature.

As I listened, a year later, to the recording of
the dialogue between my teacher, Dr. John Laird,
and me, I heard myself suddenly make the connection between my actions and an incident that had
happened two days earlier. What had transpired
was that while I was in my "safe place" working
to recover from an intense argument between us,
my husband was in my prayer room removing
anything of a spiritual nature from the shelves and
walls. When confronted with what he had done,
he could only say angrily, "I do not want God in
my house." You could have heard a pin drop in
the classroom as I spoke.*

At the time the recording was made, three
weeks had passed since the incident, yet I was

---

*   He later put the room back in order, being also
     disturbed by what he had done.

still trembling as I shared it for the first time. My anger, shame, and hurt were stronger than ever. I could not reconcile the strength of my delayed reaction with my picture of myself as a good and patient wife, nor could I accept my husband's behavior. My teacher was calm, but the class was apprehensive, as each person could relate to similar feelings in themselves.

Dr. Laird started the healing demonstration by asking me what needs of mine had not been met when my husband had dismantled my room. I named a few, such as respect, love, safety, trust, and companionship. I hoped for commiseration, but instead he proceeded to help me find those qualities for myself through the use of prayer. I was calmer after we finished, but this was only the beginning of my long spiritual trek with anger.

Listening to the tape over a year later, I heard the teacher explaining to the class things I hadn't taken in at the time, but that I now clearly understood. In so many words, the teacher was telling me that I had created a picture, a story, based on the event, and it was the *story* that had caused me such grief and anger. My story was that my husband had no respect for my religion and no love for me. As I listened a year later, I realized that the truth was that my husband had been frightened. He had been frightened he might lose me to religion, and in his panic and anger he tried to destroy the things that triggered his fears and insecurities.

Had I been more adept at recognizing and sitting with my emotions, finding my pictures and voices, and speaking from my heart, we might have reunited in love and compassion after the incident because, although I couldn't see it then, positive changes were already occurring at a deeper level. (Most likely the unrecognized stirring of change within each of us had disturbed our equilibrium and probably precipitated our extreme reactions.) However, sometimes things have to get worse before they get better. A relationship reassembled after going awry is often a stronger and more intimate one.

Victimhood: Freedom vs. Fear

Victimhood is a "poor me" state of collapse that offers false protection by creating a ready-made explanation for life events. In a state of victimhood, one's life becomes a confirmation of this expectation. *Look at how much I have to endure,* we may say. Or we may instead victimize ourselves, beating ourselves up for our failings, which is no more helpful or heroic. In either case we are victims of our beliefs. We are oppressed by our own version of reality.

Here is an example that seems ludicrous now, but illustrates the insidious power of negative beliefs. I was meeting a friend in another town at her house for lunch, and when she wasn't there at the arranged time I assumed she had forgotten our date, fully believing I had been slighted. But I recognized this false voice and, against my inclination, allowed for an alternate truth—that my friend wanted to be with me. I gave her a call and she answered right away, saying she was on her way home. Had I yielded to the voice of victimization, which I was very close to doing, I would have left an "I'm sorry I missed you" note and never had the pleasure of our lunch.

If you have been used to feeling like a victim for much of your life (as a child you may well have been victimized) you may routinely make and voice negative assumptions: for example saying to your spouse, "*Well, I guess we're never going to get a vacation this year.*" Your inner voice is telling you that your spouse *never listens to you* or that *you deserve better.* You no longer have any positive expectations regarding your relationship, so what does it matter what you say? This is a dangerous situation when your actions toward your spouse become based on your negative voices (and/or the negative voices of others), and the voices become the false truths that guide your decision-making. Unless you can see anew, your marriage can easily spiral downward into a state of disharmony. (Don't take the "*you*" personally—this happens to all of us.)

When I first had an inkling of what it felt like to *not* be the victim in a presumed hardship, it felt wonderful. I arrived there through the meeting of effort and grace, and at that moment realized that regardless of the difficulty of a situation I *always have a choice* whether or not to be a victim. To choose not to be a victim means to override the demeaning voice by listening to a voice that is more helpful, one that is more supportive of you and more generous toward others. As my counselor continually advises, "Don't take it personally."

It used to be that when I sought counseling, I always began in a state of victimhood, although I never recognized it. I might be feeling miserable because of the voice *I'm not getting what I need in my relationship.* Such voices come from the *"I-want-what-I-want"* (ego) part of my self. Usually I had read or heard about some husband doing such and such for his wife and so *I wanted that too*; it boiled down to dissatisfaction with what I had or, in other words, a lack of appreciation. Of course it is okay to have wants, but our wants are not always met, and therefore they need to be tempered with wisdom and patience.

If I stay in that place of feeling deprived long enough, as I used to do, darker voices of hate and negativity tag along, creating a constellation of negativity. It is evident these aren't the voices of truth because when I am able to release them, immense love and gratitude immediately flow into my heart, confirming the fact that the love is always there, if the veils to it can be lifted.

Victimhood is a choice. Self-responsibility is a better choice. By staying fully present to your body and your emotions, while grounding in your source of inner strength through spiritual practices, you will be better able to avoid victimhood in times of difficulty. When you choose not to be a victim, the world will naturally reflect back to you greater beauty, safety, peace, and love.

3

Self-Healing

Yesterday I sent a message as clear
and steady as a star.

You that turn stoniness to gold,
change me.

I showed you the longing and rocked
my own chest like an infant to hush it
from crying.

Undo your breast.
Take me back to love's first place
Where we were in union.[1]

The process of self-healing—i.e. addressing your feelings and needs and being open to God's grace—has a ripple effect that is far reaching. As you feel and release the hurts of your heart, you will begin to uncover and radiate the jewel of your innate nature.

What Is Self-Healing?

As the flight attendant reminds us, when the oxygen mask descends, make sure your life support is in place first before you give oxygen to another. When your heart is hurting following a relationship challenge, you must tend to *your* needs first. It is important to do this soon after your emotions have been "triggered." Though not an easy task, the solution to being free of your heart's pain is to enter directly into the places of hurt, allowing them to be doorways to your healing.

To begin the process of healing, enter your safe space to sit in the stillness and allow your feelings to flow throughout your body. (This is not easy. Our inclination is to push strong feelings away.) As you try to access your feelings, it may be difficult to distinguish feelings from voices and beliefs. For example you may say you feel betrayed, bullied, or abandoned, but these are not feelings, but rather interpretations of another's actions. Examples of feeling words are sad, nervous, or confused (or optimistic, thrilled, and calm). Any of Marshall

Rosenberg's Nonviolent Communication (NVC) books can be very helpful in distinguishing judgment, from feeling, from need. It is useful to keep a list of feelings on hand, as well as a list of needs (both from Rosenberg's books) to help you more specifically identify what you are experiencing.

If it was an argument that instigated the feelings, *try not to get stuck in obsessive thoughts* about what your spouse "did to you": i.e., apportioning blame. These feelings you are now having were already inside of you, most likely since childhood. Someone you care about simply hit the wrong button, intentionally or not, but *they did not give you the feeling*. This is an important distinction to make.

> *"Witness your emotions and turn inward inviting God into this place (of hurt) until you realize that you are responsible for all of it. This is the deepest humility."*[2]

As you *sit with your emotions*, if thoughts enter your mind dismiss them and return to the feelings of your heart. Negative thoughts about yourself, your spouse, or your future together will take you away from acknowledging and being with what you feel inside. Whether you are angry, frustrated, or sad, allow the energy of your feelings to flow throughout your body. Neither deny your feelings nor let them completely take you over, but rather be an empathetic witness to your heart.

Resist your temptation to call someone to share your troubles with. You can more quickly and fully recover if you truly face what you are feeling and invite healing into that place. *Feel the feeling.* Pray for surrender and release of whatever feeling is blocking your access to peace within, and your discomfort *will* dissipate, *inshallah.* As you stay with this process you may find that you feel revitalized, as the energy that was previously tied up in suppressing your emotions becomes newly available.

Check in with your body as well, because it is an excellent barometer for your feelings, reflecting the degree of peace or turmoil that is in your heart through its varying and subtle states of expansion (relaxation) and constriction (tension). Observe whether there is any place in your body that feels tight and put your hand there, breathing into that place. Ask this part of your body what it would tell you if it could speak: i.e., what the voice is behind your feeling. This may sound strange, but go with the first words that enter your mind. Your throat, for example, may feel an urgency to speak a truth, your neck or lower back may complain about all the burdens you carry, your stomach may express fear or insecurity, and so forth.

Some persons find it helpful to *dialogue* with their voices, as you would with your inner child, giving assurances that the adult in you can now provide the support and safety that is needed. Others prefer to talk out loud, letting all the negative voices have their say, until clarity comes.

As the voices come, using meditation, chanting, breath, and/or prayer, *allow peace, compassion, and love into those places of constriction.** Let yourself return to that still, quiet place of peace and wisdom your soul remembers.

A *supplication,* or short prayer in which one calls to God for help from a place of surrender and humility, can be very powerful: e.g., *Dear Lord, I am in great need of You; help me to find You in this prayer;* or, *Dear Lord, I seek refuge in You from my dark thoughts. Help me to hold tight to Your lifeline and Your Truth.*

Ibn' ata' Allah al-Iskandari, in his *Book of Illumination,* beautifully and clearly describes how to be fully present to a challenge and how to release it when it is over:

> *Realize that the eternal One places you in a circumstance in order that you take something from the circumstance rather than having the circumstance take something from you. Circumstance comes upon you bearing a gift for you: the potential for you to gain new knowledge about God. So turn to face each new circumstance uttering the name of the One Who initiates. Enter each changing circumstance and remain*

---

*   In NVC terms, you identify the *needs* beneath your feelings, and turn to God for their provision.

until you have received the gifts that it bears for you. Stay respectfully attentive and cultivate proper comportment while it faces you, turning your whole attention toward it. Recognize when it is beginning to pass away and, uttering the name of the One Who calls to return, return it to where it came from and let it expire.

Let's examine practically how to use the self-healing approach when your spouse's words hurt your heart. Your first reaction is an immediate *ouch.* This is the tipping point. You can focus on your spouse's behavior and go into blame mode, or you can ask yourself how you feel, why you may have reacted so strongly to what he or she said or did, and what your heart really needs. Remember, the same action may *not* have caused someone else to retreat in pain, so the reaction is a revelation about yourself. Your reaction can be an excuse to shut down your heart *or* an opportunity for learning. So, follow *ouch* with gratitude, and then the prayer *Please help me to bear this feeling and see the teaching that lies within.*

Each person will develop his or her own strategies for moving through and beyond painful thoughts and feelings. A friend of mine recently shared how she finds release for a recurring voice. When she becomes stressed from the voice *"There isn't enough time!"* she goes to her safe place, and sits with her heart. She recognizes that her stress is being fueled by this voice. She is aware of the still-held pictures of certain traumatic childhood events, events in which time was a critical issue. However, she does not dwell on the memories; because of her spiritual work, the events themselves no longer hold much emotional power for her. She allows the voice to have its say and, as she goes deeper inside, she is able to hear a more authentic voice, which is usually something like *"I need to spend more time with myself."* Choosing to listen to that more helpful voice, she determines to take some moments each day to just be with herself and listen to her heart.

Learning to discern the voice of guidance—e.g. *take some time for yourself*—from the panicked *ego* voice, *there isn't enough time*, has been an enormous help for her. Through engaging in the process of self-healing, she has come to recognize sooner when she is acting out of fear and to find the confidence and skills to work her way back into a state of trust. Because she has acquired numerous tools for self-healing, she now leads a productive and satisfying life, having once lived in a nearly constant state of fear.

My older sister takes a different course of action when she goes into overwhelm. She walks out the front door, which she says reminds her that there is a bigger picture she can access than the one she is currently seeing. In her words, she does this when she feels *separated from herself, from peace, from char-*

ity, from grace. She walks downtown, the walking itself reminding her of the beauty in the ordinary. When she sees other people she feels connected to the rest of humanity, and remembers that she is but "a grain of sand" in the infinite universe. With this larger, more humbling perspective, she then returns home, but "*not to the same place*" that she left.

These descriptions underscore that self-healing may not look the same for all of us, but that the goal is the same: i.e., that of becoming free of discomforting voices, pictures, and emotions, and entering into a larger, more peaceful place inside.

Be patient with the process. It is best to measure progress in terms of the time it takes for you to recover from an adverse incident, rather than the degree to which you can eliminate troubling incidents. In all likelihood you will never stop being triggered, but your recovery time may shorten considerably.

Dealing with Anger

A person's anger seldom has to do with the issue at hand, but rather with his or her need for love, even though angry words drive love away. Sometimes love is so scary to a person that their behavior defies others to love them, pushing them away so as to avoid the pain of loving and being loved. The truth is, no one's anger is really about the other person, but is rather about his or her own wounding.

In some instances, a partner may unconsciously push his or her spouse to the point that the spouse feels the very pain that the confronter cannot face inside his or her own being.[3] If you are on the receiving end of your spouse's anger, and can allow yourself to acknowledge and feel the part in you that carries a similar pain, you may finally come to empathize with the wounding in your spouse's heart. This is one of the highest levels of spiritual walking in a marriage. This is not a simple task, because the feelings you are accessing may be hidden and strong, but it is a pathway to healing the deepest wounds in you and in the relationship.[*]

Your task is not to seek for love, but merely to seek and find all the barriers within yourself that you have built against it.
—*Jalal ad-Din Rumi*

When you find and clean your heart of your own blocks to love, such as anger, through the principles of self-healing, there will be no place for the hostility of others to stick because there will be nothing inside you to resonate with their

---

[*]   This is not to say that all behavior is to be condoned. Clearly spouses must endeavor to be in the *adab* (polite) with one another. Page 65 of this book describes a process for expressing one's needs clearly and compassionately.

anger. Then, *inshallah*, you will be able to hold a loving presence for your spouse, and others, without judgment, regardless of the strength of their emotions.

For most of us, however, there still remain places inside where harsh words can hurt. In this case it is helpful to view the moments when you are triggered not as insult to your person but as a validation that you are ready to address your wounding. In this way, the anger of another may become fuel for your growth.

To review, what steps do you take to recover from being triggered by someone's anger?

- Gently excuse yourself to your place of refuge. As difficult as it may be, stay with your feelings and avoid listening to the voices that tell you, *this marriage isn't working,* or, *if only he/she would just do such and such my life would be much better.*

- *Whenever your mind wanders* to your husband or wife, *return to your feelings. Stay* with your feelings. Additional feelings may come up, such as anxiety, anger, confusion, fatigue, or embarrassment. Be present to those as well.

- "If you find yourself in a state of anger, then stand if you were sitting, and if you were standing, then sit down." If your anger does not go away, splash cold water on your face or take a cool shower.[4]

- Say *no* to the unhelpful voices after giving them their say. Listen for your Higher Guidance.

- If your voices stubbornly remain, use prayer, breath, chanting, imagery, or whatever helps you enter a peaceful place where there are no voices or where they have no power.

- As you navigate your inner self you may be reminded of feelings from other situations that are still affecting you. Perhaps you are worried about one of your children or are still hurting from a coworker's remarks. Or, likely, some childhood event also accompanies your feelings. Attend to all the thoughts and feelings that tag along, until they lose some of their charge.

- *Ask yourself what your heart needs.* It may be that you are in need of greater love, companionship, or peace (or predictability, safety, mutuality, fairness, etc.).

- *Allow yourself to feel remorse* for the separation you feel, because of your reaction, from God, from your best nature, and from your spouse. *Let God's Mercy flow in.*

- *Stay with your heart's longing* until you feel some relief. Positive imagery and prayer may be helpful for bringing in the qualities you need (e.g., peace, love).

- When your own needs have been substantially met (through connection to God and your

inner wisdom) and you have released any
blame you feel toward your spouse, return to
your spouse and let him or her know, silently
or in a few words, that you wish to reconnect.*

This describes the process of listening to and
taking responsibility for your feelings, and of trac-
ing various emotions to their root feeling. Over
time, rather than numerous separate problems and
hassles in your life, which can seem insurmount-
able, you will come to recognize that there are
but *one or two root modes of feeling* that cause you
suffering. If you stay the course with these feelings, recognizing and clearing the accompanying
voices, *you will no longer be at the mercy of the events
in your life.* True freedom comes from knowing
that whatever life throws at you, you can safely
navigate the pain and emerge from the experience
with greater strength, peace, and self-knowledge.

Seeking Help

Help from someone else may be necessary when
your feelings, voices, and/or pictures become too
strong for you to bear alone. The rule of thumb is
that forty-eight hours is long enough to be stuck in
negative voices or emotions. Seek the listening ear

---

*   More on speaking from your heart can be found in
     chapter 4 of this book.

of a spiritual counselor if you are still in turmoil.

Here are some traits you want to look for in a counselor:

- A person who is empathetic and can hold your heart from a place of love, peace, and strength.
- A person who directs you to your heart, rather than the repetition of your story or beliefs.
- Someone who is not disturbed by strong feelings and knows that addressing feelings is the doorway to healing.
- A person who encourages self-responsibility: i.e., redirects your focus from your spouse or boss, etc., back to yourself.
- Someone who knows a variety of spiritual tools that can fill your heart's needs and will help you practice the ones you are drawn to.

I have gratitude for the many counselors who have helped me to look more clearly at myself. However, one particular interchange was very helpful in helping me understand anger. My counselor told me that my problem was *not* that my husband was not loving, but rather that *I had difficulty receiving* love. At that point the words from one of my USHS teachers came back to me: *"He's just trying to break down the door to your heart."* As my counselor worked with me, she helped me begin to open my heart, even gently rapping on my chest during one healing. *People only attack those who carry swords or shields*, she told me, and she helped me to lay down my shield.

Surrendering

Resistance to life as it presents to us can lead to spiritual torment if we lack the tools for gentling our egos. There is a transformative moment in the novel *The Horse Whisperer*, by Nicholas Evans, in which a wounded and terrified horse is finally healed. The horse whisperer forces the trembling horse to the ground, and when the horse finally submits to the man, his fear is released and he is calm at long last. This is the way it works for all of us. *When we finally give up our fight against something in our lives that we cannot change, and decide that we are willing to accept what is, even if we feel it is more than we can bear, we may find, through grace, a sense of deep peace and even a transformation of circumstance.*

When the Prophet Abraham was asked to sacrifice his son, he was being asked, symbolically, if he trusted God enough to sacrifice that which he cared for the most. Was he willing to put God first? His son, who was coming of age, was also being asked the same question. *Both* of them fully surrendered to God's will. However, when Abraham raised his knife to follow God's request, the knife turned to water, according to some references, because it was their complete *willingness to surrender*, not the actual sacrifice, that God wanted.

Next time you are certain that you were not meant to live in this neighborhood, or be in this marriage, or have that mother, feel into that dense place inside you that is fighting acceptance of what you have been given. Resistance can be a powerful, even obsessive, force. *Sacrifice your certainty* about what you think you need in order to move into a place of acceptance for what you have been given. God may have even better plans for you than you can imagine.

The fastest way through a trial is to fully embrace it. This is not to say that one should put up with abuse or that one cannot switch jobs, houses, or towns. But with difficult and unavoidable situations, such as living in a town you don't love, having quadruplets when you expected only a single child, or being in a volatile marriage, your biggest lessons and gifts will come from releasing your resistance to what is. Surrender, ask a Higher Power for help, and give it your best shot.

If you cannot do this, then pray for help in surrendering. My roommate at school had only one answer to my every complaint: "Well, there's your next prayer!" Praying for the release of an unwanted trait, such as judgment of others, opens the door for its release, in time.

There are ever-deepening levels of surrender

in a marriage. Many partners leave the back door ajar, that is to say they hold on to the option of leaving, if the relationship should become too difficult. But the irony is that locking the back door and standing firm in your marriage is only way to find the deep love you desire. As a friend recently shared with me, "I waited twenty-five years to shut the back door in my marriage, thinking that my freedom was in leaving a safety net, but the irony was that I only truly felt safe when I shut the back door and didn't look back." Statistics regarding arranged marriages, for example, where there is no contemplation of separation, indicate that such marriages do as well as, if not better than, traditional marriages. For myself, I know that each time I committed more deeply to my marriage, there was a corresponding ease in my relationship, and each time I glanced toward the back door, the challenges increased.

For many years I held a part of me back, waiting, not merely for the marriage to become easier, but to find the guidance as to whether being in this marriage was what was truly being asked of me. Because of the strong challenges, I thought perhaps that my teaching was about how to leave, in order to protect my heart. I resisted bowing to the marriage and all that would entail, until one moment, while listening to a teaching on Abraham, I clearly saw the truth that there was great goodness and honor in surrendering to God's will. *When I closed the back door, everything changed.*

Accepting my marriage, and whatever it might bring me, freed me to look more honestly at my husband, at both his easy and challenging qualities. I found greater freedom to be my true self and to allow him to do the same. Our successes and struggles became of less import, as the marriage no longer hinged on any one event, but rather was held in the container of my willingness to accept my husband for all time. With acceptance came greater appreciation of the marriage and, not surprisingly, peace began to permeate our home.

For some people, deep commitment may come naturally, but for myself it was a struggle. For others who may also be struggling, I include the following prayer, which came to me in the night:

> *Dear Lord, I have spent long hours seeking guidance regarding my marriage. I have asked for ease, and still I struggle, sometimes to the limits of my endurance. I feel trapped, but I now realize that I am in a prison of my own making. My resistance is the cause of my suffering. I have read of the great burdens of the saints and the prophets, of good men and women, and their acceptance of difficulty with faith and humility, and I see now the holiness of surrendering to that which I have been given.*

I am shutting the back door in this marriage.
I fully embrace my husband, my marriage, and
whatever challenges may come. Please help me
see through new eyes the beauty and majesty
of marriage and deepen my gratitude for this
union. I trust in Your wisdom and protection
and pledge henceforth to live in the truth of my
surrender.
Amen.

Forgiveness

The quality of mercy is not strain'd,
It droppeth as the gentle rain from heaven
Upon the place beneath.
It is twice blest:
It blesseth him that gives and him that takes.
—The Merchant of Venice,
    Act 4, Scene 1, 180–187

Forgiveness for ourselves, then others, prepares our heart to open more fully to love. We must strive to release our judgment about what others have done. We are not the dispensers of justice or truth, but are held responsible only for our own actions. Each person is allowed the same opportunities as we are, to mess up, to learn from mistakes, and to receive mercy. As Byron Katie writes in *Loving What Is, there are three orders of business: someone else's business, God's business, and your business, and only the last one need concern you.*

It takes only one person to release a grudge. That is because when we let go of *our* resentment, there is no place in us for the other's resentment to resonate. When we return to be with the person, with no hard feelings, they usually welcome us back without our ever having to say a word. This is a reminder that it is what is in our heart, not on our lips, that is transmitted to others.

A MEDITATION[*]

Close your eyes, and think of something or someone you love. It could be a tree, a person, an animal, or whatever or whomever at this moment evokes love in your heart.

Be fully with the feeling of love; consider all aspects of that love, letting it become more and more expansive.

Now feel only the love. Bathe in the feeling of love, with your heart and your senses. Perhaps you feel tingly or warm, see light, or feel like you have come home at last.

Now allow yourself to feel the healing energy emanating from the love. As you tap into this energy, allow love and healing to flow throughout your body and overflow to your surroundings.

---

[*]   Adapted from an exercise led by Dr. John Laird of USHS.

4

Opening to Love

Love everything to know what
love means.
You need to be born again and again
in the garden of love. Love and love
and love because there is no life with-
out the love and no meaning without
the love.[1]

Love

Love is transformative. There is no end to the amount of love you can embrace, but at each level of walking, you will come up against places where you say, *this is enough for now, I can hold no more love.* Your heart can physically hurt when it expands in love. Yet, each barrier to love will, in time, dissolve, if you keep love ever as your goal.

Do you ever experience being filled with love for your mate when he or she is gone, only to have your love decrease when your husband or wife returns home? This is because his or her human qualities and your expectations veil your love, but the love itself is no less real for that. Your falling in love was a gift, ignited *by* your spouse, but promising connection to an even greater love, divine love.

Know, my beloved, that the love is eternal between God and His creation and the electric circuitry of His love flows through everything. If not for this, nothing would move that moves; nothing would live that lives. Every planet in its orbit and every cell in its course is a witness to the love of God and a sign of His wisdom. Keep this love inside you and live with it all the time because the moment you lose it, you lose yourself; you lose God.[2]

How is it you stay together as a couple even in the toughest of times? It is because love is so resilient, so powerful, and so holy. Your beings recognize on some level that the love you have for one another is your surest connection to God's Love, and so you will not let go of love lightly.

Staying present to the essence of the love

between you allows a bigger container for your marriage. In this expansive ocean of love and mercy, a more intimate connection can be experienced, one that is shared in silence and even physical separation.

If you remember that the love between you and your spouse is strong, being at its essence divine, then when your relationship becomes turbulent you will recognize that it is only because you *turned away from the abiding love and its Source*. Be vigilant to the love that first connected you, rather than to your spouse's outward behavior. Remember, as soon and as often as you can, to return from dissatisfaction to gratitude and from judgment to love. In this way, over time, you will *become the earth for one another*, not by letting your hearts be trampled, but by providing the secure ground in which your partner's heart can rest.

Speaking from Your Heart

Sometimes you really need to speak your mind and heart. But how can this be done with grace? From a state of serenity and love you can speak your feelings and/or make a sincere request, with no blame or expectation, and your spouse will listen.

In difficult interactions, employ the American Indian fourfold way: show up, pay attention, speak your truth, and detach from outcome. Being able to do this begins with taking responsibility for your feelings. Take your negative feelings to God, not your spouse, until you can feel love in your heart again. Then, if you have returned to a state of peace and still feel the need to speak, do so, gently.

Here is a helpful procedure I developed for speaking to my spouse when our emotions were extremely high. The resulting brevity and authenticity of my choice of words enabled me both to understand and to express my needs. I cannot underestimate the value of its use in establishing clarity and communication.

- Plan your words so that you can be brief, and concise. *Distill what you want to say into just two to four sentences.* This is an extremely helpful exercise in itself, as you may not know exactly what you are feeling or what your needs are. Don't rush the process. Stick to how you *feel* and what you *need*, rather than any comments about your spouse.
- Acknowledge the value of yourself and what you have to say.
- Release all blame, judgment, and resentment toward your spouse, using your spiritual practices to do that.
- Release any shame or guilt you may have for your feelings, in the same manner.
- Know, from the deepest part of your being, that your feelings are entirely your own, and

were not fostered upon you by any actions of your partner.

- Believe that you, not your partner, have full responsibility for taking care of your feelings.
- Be in complete detachment from the outcome, your only goal being to speak your truth.
- Practice speaking, modifying your sentences until you feel certain that your words express the essence of what you need to say, *and that you are speaking from a place that will not hurt your spouse's heart.*
- Secure your spouse's attention, through eye contact and physical proximity and asking please to share a few sentences that are weighing on your heart.
- Be *polite.* Be *soft.* Speak *gently.* Limit yourself only to the prepared sentences.
- After speaking, remain open and silent, *releasing all expectations* of how you think your spouse will or should respond.
- Continue to stay with your partner for a few minutes, being present to your feelings and being open to whatever follows.

(The same process will work for bigger concerns, though you may not be able to distill your thoughts into three or four sentences. However, you will probably find several components to what you need to say, and so can use the process of brevity with each component.)

Here are three separate examples of speaking from the heart taken from my own experience, followed by one shared by a classmate of mine (with permission to print):

- *I'm really sad. I feel hopeless when we argue in the mornings.*
- *When you leave home without speaking to me my heart always hurts. When you explain why you are leaving and where you are going, I am able to accept this and I feel safe.*
- *I was frightened when I heard you say ___ because I thought it might mean that you were thinking ____. I was afraid we might begin to lose all the gains we have made.*

The next, and last, example, put in an email to a potential suitor, led to a sweet outcome. The woman who wrote it worked with me one evening at USHS, applying my Speaking from the Heart process, as I needed to prepare for a class teaching the next day. She wanted to craft a somewhat overdue response to an email, written to her some months earlier by a male friend, asking her if she was interested in a romantic relationship. As we worked together that evening, she eventually found the words that were in her heart and sent them off by email that night.

She opened with, *I am now on the Land and a bit more clear.*

Here are the four sentences she spent an hour clarifying:

My heart is terrified of love and yet ready for it.

I seek a relationship with two hearts sharing their journey to God.

My heart is open to you.

When you are not in relationship I am open to explore this.

After she sent the email she told me that *she did not even feel the need for a response,* because she had felt such relief in finding and speaking her truth.

When I saw her six months later, she was moving to be closer to her new beloved, the one whom she had emailed, a man she eventually married!

In short, to discern when to speak, assess your state of being, rather than the time of day or the mood of your partner. Speak when your heart can "give the clean water"; i.e. speak with kindness, truth, and love. You will know that you were ready because *when you speak it will feel right.* If you are hesitant to speak, most likely you are not yet clear about your motive, your words, or your detachment from blame or shame. Wait until you have worked that through. Perhaps when you are ready there will no longer even be a need to speak, as the situation will have resolved itself as a result of your inner work.

Be merciful with yourself. Speaking from the heart takes a lot of work and practice; but when you bravely bring your *truth with love* into moments of potential separation, it opens the possibility that a misunderstanding can bring your hearts closer together, rather than drive them further apart.

My experience is that when I speak cleanly, with no expectation or accusation, my spouse has no need to defend himself and therefore is free to hear and to help me. When I can speak from my heart, and step out of my judgment and need for change, I learn acceptance for situations that were once intolerable. And sometimes, as my counselor long advised me to do, I even find our struggles humorous and our foibles endearing.

Just Say *Yes*

A wise woman once told me that love means giving your spouse what he or she wants even if you don't understand why. When your spouse makes *a request that you are able to comply with*, your judgment may cause you to resist; you think you should understand and/or approve of your spouse's need before you give of yourself. In your mind you may

be thinking, *That's ridiculous; no one should need that!*
Knowing as you do now that your spouse has different wounds, needs, and goals, it makes sense to
honor each sincere request, if you have the means
to do so. Saying *yes* to your spouse affirms your
love and acceptance of his or her unique way of
being and is essential medicine for *his or her* heart.
Being generous of spirit is medicine for *your* heart.

Looking Through the Eye of Your Heart

In marriage, it is easy to miss the love your spouse
is giving to you in simple actions such as putting
up a hook for you in the bedroom closet or gently
closing the cabinet door you left open. The very
act of coming home to you every evening is an
act of faith and devotion that is often taken for
granted. When not seeing through soft eyes, you
may overlook the spiritual component to lovemak-
ing, seeing it with eyes clouded by the assumption
that your spouse is only driven by physical need.
Empty your mind of all preconceptions and open
them to the probability that your spouse's gestures
are motivated by love, whether gifts to you in his
or her own currency of love, or cries from a heart
seeking or running from love. Seeing love behind
each gesture fosters kindness and reverence in a
marriage.

Be the Container

Being the container for your spouse describes a state in which your heart is large enough to hold your spouse in love, peace, and mercy, no matter what he or she is saying or doing. To *contain* another person is to "*hold them as precious*," one of my teachers said. That really stuck with me. Hold your self as precious first, and then you will be able to hold your spouse as precious. Within this expansive and loving container, your marriage will naturally heal.

Protecting Your Inner Self

Safeguard your inner "jewel." Intimacy cannot be forced. Your partner may not be ready for you to share the details of your inner journey, now, or ever. When deep sharing comes, it is a beautiful gift that allows both hearts to enter into the same sacred space. Be grateful for the gift, but not attached to its coming or going, for you can always find the peace and connection you seek within your own being. Moreover, *do not assume that you know all of what is being shared unspoken between you and your spouse.* Be assured that communication and bonding are happening on a deep level simply through the continued sharing of time and space.

The Different Needs of Men and Women

Although this book was written for either partner, one cannot ignore the fact that men and women often have differing human needs and spiritual inclinations. (The books of Patricia Love and John Gray are helpful references in this regard.) As a result of her research with fifteen hundred couples, Patricia Love writes in her book *How to Improve Your Marriage Without Talking About It* that "Most women do not understand how much it pleases a man to please a woman." and, "Furthermore a man does not simply want to please her—he *lives* to please her." Love and Gray would probably agree that, in general, men need to be accepted and to make women happy, and are prone to guilt and shame when they feel they have failed at this. For this reason, a woman's criticism can break the love connection between husband and wife.

To the women—let your husband be the one to comfort you, *even if you believe him to be the source of your pain*. Find a way to let your husband be the hero. Ask him sweetly to hold you because your heart is in pain and you know he is the only one who can help. You will be surprised how healing this approach is. After all, he doesn't want to think he hurt you, but he wants ever so much to be the one to make it better.

While both men and women need emotional connection, women tend to more actively seek it out. Thus, a woman may be more upset by harsh words, her own or her spouse's, because they break her emotional connection with her spouse.

To the men — Take time to be kind to your wife, even if you may have made a mistake and spoken in a manner that appears to have hurt her heart. Men have much to gain by learning to speak gently and by appreciating the spiritual pole that the wife holds. If you cannot speak, then just hold her until you can feel her heart soften.

Spiritually speaking, the woman holds the peace, mercy, and compassion for the man. She is the home base into which he enters. This makes sense, as women carry the seeds of future generations and so are given the gift of greater ease in carrying deep love and divine connection, but to be this in a deep way she must clean her heart.

The woman is said to carry the heart of the marriage, or, as John Gray writes in *Why Mars and Venus Collide*, "Women are the custodians of love, family, and relationship.... When women are not happy, no one is happy."

If these differing needs are not taken into account, it is easy to see how difficulties arise that, if ignored, can create an ever widening rift between spouses. For example, when a woman is critical of her husband, he may become defensive and withdraw; then she will also suffer, having lost her connection with her spouse. The woman, however, by owning her need for connection, can gently seek out her husband and help to mend the separation.

Conversely, when a man deprives his wife of connection through harsh words, she may withdraw her love to protect her heart, and her husband, feeling responsible for her sadness, may also withdraw. But when he owns his need for pleasing his wife, instead of retreating he can do things that help her return to the love and, in so doing, receive the love he needs.

Optimally, in light of these theories, when a wife loves her husband unconditionally, she reflects back to him his highest self and he can find his divine connection, and peace, through her heart. When a man gives to his wife the safety and emotional connection that she needs, her heart will open wider in love for him, and she, too, will find peace.

The work of feeding one another's hearts is holy work, so honor one another's deepest needs. A relationship between two egos gains nothing, but the intimacy between two hearts and two souls carries the potential for unity.

Trust Your Progress

There will naturally be backsliding and challenges in your walking. As a rule, when you've learned something big and moved into a new and better place in your marriage, a test will *inevitably* come, strengthening your new skills and showing you where you are in relation to your new learning. Be patient and merciful regarding your progress. Reflect, now and then, on how far you've come and how many of the things that once worried you have dropped away. Perseverance in love will transform you and your marriage, even if not as you imagined. Keep your focus on your inner landscape and trust that your relationship will evolve toward its intended perfection, *through love*.

Afterword

Every relationship is a reflection of our relationship with God. Let us return to remembrance of God as deeply and as often as we can, for in that connection we will find contentment, peace, love, wisdom, and the full treasure of divine qualities that is our essence and our inheritance.

I wish for you blessings and peace on your journey. May your longing for love and your yearning to rest in the arms of your Lord keep you steadfast on your spiritual path. May your marriage continually be showered with the clean water of love, *inshallah*.

Salima Sanford

Appendix A: Troubleshooting

The act of writing can ground you during tough times. After a difficult situation has passed you might benefit from recording your observations, thoughts, feelings, and needs, and whatever tool you used to return to peace of mind. *This may help you to understand any repetitive patterns, remember what worked and what didn't, and gain confidence in your progress.*

Begin with your complaint. For example:

THE SITUATION: I'm feeling crabby and I want more attention from my spouse. I want him to make me feel better in my irritability and thus I continue to seek his attention.

Awareness: The truth is that I'm no longer attending to myself and this is the cause of my crabbiness. I'm looking solely to my husband to provide for my psychological and spiritual needs.

The Way Out: Once I'm aware of what I'm doing, instead of seeking his attention I take time to be with myself, using whatever tools I have to find the peace and sustenance I need. When I return, less needy, my husband gives more freely from his heart.

The Learning: When I'm needy for attention, I most likely need to spend time with myself first, to return to the awareness that the true source of peace is inside my own being.

THE SITUATION: I don't feel love and I don't feel loved.

Awareness: I'm not accepting what my husband offers to me as love. I'm being given love but I don't recognize it as such, because it's not in the manner I want.

The Way Out: I rekindle the love in my heart through my practices. I consciously notice, receive, and appreciate the love my spouse is giving.

The Learning: By returning to the love in my heart, I can more easily receive love, in whatever manner it is given.

THE SITUATION: I am judgmental of my husband. I am stuck in negative thinking and his behavior becomes ever-more irritating.

Awareness: My judgment is turning me from love. I'm making a picture about my husband that may not even be true. I am missing the teaching that my frustration can provide.

The Way Out: I look within to clean within that which I am seeing on the outside. I pray for release of judgment.

The Learning: My negative thinking needs to be dealt with quickly, through my practices. My husband's behavior will become sweeter when the lens through which I see him is sweeter.

THE SITUATION: I'm thinking our marriage is in a rut, and becoming impatient with our progress.

Awareness: Intimacy ebbs and flows. Perhaps this is a time for integration following a period of growth in our marriage.

The Way Out: I work to let go of my pictures of what a relationship should look like, and strive to accept the relationship as it is. I let go of any time frame I have for greater intimacy.

The Learning: My expectations for marriage limit the reality of what marriage can become, which may be something far more beautiful than I can imagine.

Looking over your notes may be useful when you find yourself cycling through familiar patterns of disconnection.

As the experience of peace and love between you and your spouse becomes the norm rather than the exception, you will not settle for the return of discord and separation. Having new hope, you will do whatever is needed to reconnect, *inshallah*.

Appendix B:
Ten Steps to Healing

1. Surrender to, rely on, and be in dialogue with your Higher Power.
2. Accept that everything you see is from you and for you. Let go of judgment of others, whatever their state, for each person has his/her own walking.
3. Use life events, whether harsh or sweet, as your teachers.
4. Do not blame others, but rather take full responsibility for your reactions to outer events. Release your restrictive images of people and events, accepting the incomprehensibility of God's manifestation in others. Leave guilt and shame behind, turning instead to the voices that make you feel good.
5. Find tools and resources that enable you to face your pain, knowing your feelings are but

doorways through which you can find greater strength, peace, and knowledge.

6. From your place of greater wholeness, self-responsibility, humility, and grace, discern when and how to speak your truth.

7. Observe your walking. There will be times for rest and integration, times for striving and being in the world. Measure your progress by your recovery time when you are triggered. Be patient and merciful with yourself. Expect trials and setbacks.

8. Surrender to Allah but tether your camel. Bow to whatever God makes for you. Seek guidance from your Creator for wise action.

9. Want for others what you want for yourself.

10. Open your being to receive the infinite love, mercy, and guidance available from God in every moment through every facet of creation.

Notes

Chapter 1

1. From "The Hope of Loving" by Meister Eckhart, in Daniel Ladinsky, *Love Poems from God* (New York: Penguin, 2002).
2. This activity is adapted from Craig and Amy Carpentieri, *His and Her Toolkit: Practical Tools for Rebuilding Your Relationship* (Createspace, 2007), chapter 1.
3. Ibid.
4. Shaykh Muhammad Sa'id Al-Jamal ar-Rifa'i as-Shadhuli, *He Who Knows Himself, Knows His Lord* (Sidi Muhammad Press, 2007), 105.
5. Amal E. Jamal, *Jewels of Hope* (IQRA International Education Foundation, 2008).
6. Kahlil Gibran, *The Prophet* (New York: Knopf, 2000), 12.

Chapter 2

1. From a teaching by Yahya Howard on the *adab* (deep politeness).

2. Shaykh Muhammad Sa'id Al-Jamal ar-Rifa'i as-Shadhuli, *Music of the Soul* (Sidi Muhammad Press, 2007), 220.

Chapter 3

1. From Jalāl ad-Dīn Rumi, "I Rocked My Own Chest," in Coleman Barks, *Rumi: Bridge to the Soul* (New York: Harper, 2007).

2. Quoted from a teaching on the *adab*, by Yahya Howard.

3. Recollection from reading: Patricia Evans, The Verbally Abusive Relationship (Holbrook MA: Adams Media Corporation, 2003).

4. Shaykh Muhammad Sa'id Al-Jamal ar-Rifa'i as-Shadhuli, *He Who Knows Himself, Knows His Lord*, 86.

Chapter 4

1. Shaykh Muhammad Sa'id Al-Jamal ar-Rifa'i as-Shadhuli, *Music of the Soul* (Sidi Muhammad Press, 2007), 85, 91.

2. Ibid., 173.

About the Author

Salima Linda holds a Masters of Divinity degree from the University of Spiritual Healing and Sufism (2009). She is a passionate student of Sufism and healing.

Salima is a respected Muqqadim Murabbi in her Shadhdhuliyyah Sufi community, both locally and nationally, dedicated to holding the hearts of others, and guiding them on their spiritual path. She trained under Dr. Robert Jaffe as Master Healer and has been a healer, mentor, and teacher for many years, working individually and with groups, in person, by phone, and through Skype/Zoom. Since June 2010, she has been the lead teacher for her second group of Institute of Spiritual Healing students.

Her Sufi name is derived from the quality *Salaam*, meaning peace, safety, and wholeness. *Salim* is often translated as "river of peace." She creates a safe and peaceful space for her clients, enabling them to find their divine, inviolable place of goodness, truth, and strength within, and to pass through the doorway of each challenge, however difficult, into the light of healing of mind, body, heart, and spirit.

Salima's second book, *Nurturing Love*, will be available in the fall of 2022.